IN THE ZONE

KEY WORDS THAT INSPIRE SUCCESS IN SPORTS

IN
THE ZONE

KEY WORDS THAT
INSPIRE SUCCESS IN SPORTS

A GUIDE TO WINNING
in sports and in life

BRIAN JACOBS

Brian Jacobs
72899 Skyward Way
Palm Desert, Ca.
brianjacobs77@icloud.com

CONTENTS

Brian is a tennis coach and lifelong athlete. He has spent the last 20 years coaching and mentoring players of all ages. Working alongside some of the greatest tennis coaches and mentors in the industry. From top keynote speakers to the best tennis directors and club coaches, CEO's to Celebrities, a former world #1 ATP tennis player and having a mentor in a current world champion in the men's senior ITF tennis circuit. From being in the trenches with passion driven individuals that pour their sweat and tears into the sport with dedication, desire and determination, to the many players whom have shared their own experiences overcoming challenges and learning to grow.

Learning from the best while helping his tennis students find personal and athletic growth through passion and charisma. He has built programs for city recreation departments, athletic clubs, country clubs, and coached boys and girls high school tennis for a top ranked Southern California team. A loving and devoted dad to two wonderfully talented kids, Ian and Ivy and spends much of his free time helping guide them into becoming the best they can be.

Engaging in a competitive environment creates a sense of motivation that embodies you and it's very simple - either you like it or you don't. But one thing's for sure; from this point, your journey starts. It's almost like getting a rush of energy, a euphoria ! As you start to get a taste of the excitement a vision is created. From here the question is, how far can you go ? This creates a deep motivating feeling that can lead you towards your goals and achieving them. It's in the "small achievable" goals that shelter the answers of which way to go next, ultimately giving you a direction to take. This is the road most successful people are on and are faced with a multitude of challenging situations.

The road is not easy and oftentimes forces a person to look at themselves and find out just how physically and mentally strong they are. Without question, these difficult times, also known as "roadblocks", appear along your path. Just know the main reason they are there is to test your personal growth and strength. So again, how far can you go ? Take this information, apply it to those times of struggle and suffering, stay strong and remove those certain "roadblocks" that present themselves.

This book connects realistic situations through sports, business and life while giving you helpful tools in learning how to manage the change that is needed along the way. So I welcome you on your continuing journey as you enter this phase with a new perspective, free from fear, able to express yourself while actually enjoying the process.

1

FIND THE SPACE LET YOURSELF GROW

LIFE MOVES FAST BUT SEE IF YOU
CAN EASE OFF THAT GAS PEDAL,
STEP AWAY FROM THE PUSH, SIT
BACK FROM THE PRESSURE.

As fast as the world is moving, you come to find that there is energy always present, hidden energy that is constantly asking you the question, "Do you want it?"

For now, let's slow down and actually take a deep breath without rushing it. Just stop and fill your lungs with air as you breathe in and let them fully expand. Go ahead; I'll wait........ Enjoy this moment because here you are creating a feeling of space. Get comfortable with the pause at the top of the breath and create it for yourself as you slowly exhale. This is what is called that "now moment" and in the world of sports and business there is a need to become very familiar with this special timing. It is so important to stay in the now moment and to be present and fully aware not only in your preparation, training and competitive moments but also in life outside of competition.

Okay, here we are and in this moment you have found the space. You have found the space to let yourself grow. This is the mindful and emotional space you are creating to become stronger. The more you do it, the more familiar you become with creating this in all your life and surroundings. It is a place where the journey starts. Your direction is set. Now the work begins.

FIND TIME TO LISTEN TO THE SILENCE

2

THE WORK IS DONE WHEN NO ONE IS WATCHING

I t's easy to think that extraordinary people are born with talent, that they have been blessed with an abundance of fortuity and are naturally gifted. While some of those stories might be true, there are some hidden secrets that reveal the roots of what breeds certain greatness. For example if you have strong daily routines and find a deep sense of inspiration in what you do, this can lead you to where you want to be. It's what inspires you that will breed strength and confidence. When you find the things that make you happy, you are then connected to your own intrinsic motivation to want to do the work. It is very authentic when a deep desire sparks the motivation to reach your goals. If you set your intentions high this allows for the progressive change to occur, bringing your awareness to new levels. The next step is to build on it. Start with small, achievable goals, managing the space in your personal life while you prepare for a competitive environment. Have a solid daily routine, every day reaching and working towards your goals. Much of the work is in just keeping up with the daily grind coupled with managing to steer around those inevitable "roadblocks", in whatever form they come.

The journey is filled with many different ways to go, but if you look closely enough you will see the little details that all the excellent, even most successful competitors do to stay ahead of the curve. It all comes down to this! In order for you to get better, you need to make it happen. No use in sitting around waiting for things to come, 'cause they won't.

HAVE DREAMS OF WHERE YOU WANT TO BE THIS IS WHERE THE VISION IS CREATED

Start by repetitions of lifestyle habits and daily training routines. Build a schedule for yourself and have an interest in learning as much as you can while being open for the change that comes with it. Practice thoughtful exercises such as listening to podcasts, reading and writing, sharing your experiences with friends and family and asking questions. Become eager in always seeking out information. From this, you will find those who will support you along your journey. These are the people you must surround yourself with. Stick with it and move towards your goals.

3

What is Your Daily Obsession?

IT IS YOUR BEST FRIEND. THE ONE WHO NEVER LEAVES YOU AND WILL ALWAYS BE THERE BY YOUR SIDE. IT'S YOU! IT'S YOUR VOICE, YOUR MIND, YOUR THOUGHTS, YOUR HABITS.

Character is a direct result of your obsessions. Obsessions with the "right intentions" can motivate you in becoming determined to achieve your goals. Obsessions do not need to have a negative connotation if used with the right intentions. These are the thoughts that circulate in our mind. It's all energy and we create it. In order to control the energy of what you put out, try focusing on the new energy being received and what is allowed in. The secret is in building a consistent pattern of thoughts and behaviors that are all directed at helping you achieve your goals. Do this and you will find the power of manifesting your dreams into reality.

In a world of constant pursuit to be the best, to be first, to take the lead, having discipline with a strong vision is key. Creating a vision sets the level of awareness to rise above distractions and not be sucked into the trend that takes you away from your goals.

"Virtue and purity are not rooted in weakness. Rather, they are strong qualities that fight the forces of evil . It is within your power to choose how much purity, love, beauty, and spiritual joy you will express, not only through deeds, but in your thoughts, feelings and desires . It is necessary to rouse from the deeper recesses of your consciousness the intuitive faculties of the pure soul. The power of habit is very important on the spiritual path .

(A "Para-Gram" by Paramahansa Yogananda)

PURE MIND, PURE THOUGHTS, PURE HABITS

4

FIND YOUR CENTER

SELF-DISCIPLINE IS A DAILY OBSESSION

In life and in sports and business you are faced with challenges. You learn to manage the struggle and at times are faced with the uncertainty of not knowing how to achieve your goals or if it is even possible. Handling this kind of pressure teaches us to find ourselves through the feelings of suffering and sometimes loss.

Think for a moment about a time when you felt rushed and begin to sense the pressure of a situation. The moment moves quickly and is intense. Tension is created in the body and it is at that moment you have a choice.

- *Close down and hold on to the pressure?*
- *Stay open and use it to flow into the next moment?*

Managing this type of energy through our emotions is a learned skill. It is about being totally present and having awareness and deep understanding of who you are as a person. It is about knowing how your personality reacts to things. Ask yourself this; are there times when you get too excited? Do you have a tendency to rush things? Do you feel more like a risk taker or do you take more of a conservative approach? When it is time to perform, do you feel yourself starting to sink into a pit of fear and succumb to the pressure?

When your energy is out of balance, you are either chasing something or holding on to it. Keeping a non-controlling mind and staying open to the change will allow you to feel free while staying present. But trying to use control and overpower this energy is like holding on to pressure that just keeps building and building. Over time it will collapse. Look at it this way. Emotional fire has two sides, a positive and a negative side. There are times when you get so angry that it pumps you up full of fight, wanting to win at all costs. Then again, there are times when anger and frustration set in, creating a loss of focus in this crucial time of pressure. Be clear with your direction. Stay focused and take setbacks as learning opportunities.

Create a state of balance in your mind . Find your center! Have a good perspective and learn to maintain emotional balance. 'Cause after all, to be mentally prepared means you must manage your life so that you walk into battle eager, fresh and fully ready to fight.

5

LIFE IS PASSION LIVE YOUR VISION

Passion is like a burning flame inside your heart. As soon as you touch it your whole body gets warm and filled with energy. When you begin to really "live your vision" you'll start using this flame to guide your path like a light in a dark cave. This is actually just more or less of understanding your goals and the direction it takes in achieving them.

Pay close attention to your dreams not only at night but during the day as well; this will give you some insight into what your passions really are. It's all about knowing how you want to be. If you don't know that's okay, just start with a solid daily routine while putting in the work towards growth. Keep yourself accountable in doing the work no matter how you feel. You will find "your vision" through the strength it takes to hold yourself accountable. This vision will share with you how the journey looks along the way. You will be able to see it in your dreams or in the still moments of the day when glimpsing something that captures your attention. When resting or deep in sleep, use the "power of vision" as part of your daily training and watch how life changes from a dream into reality. The mental exercise is this, (do this as you read slowly).

Sit in a quiet space for a moment. Relax and breathe deeply. Do not rush this moment but breathe with full expanding breaths. Feel your lungs expand on the inhale and fully relax into the exhale. Breathe, Breathe, Relax. Open your mind and feel what the heart desires. What do you love? What you are chasing? This is the moment where the intention is created and it will be the backbone of the dream. Sit for a moment in this power. "Listen to the silence" as this is the space where the vision is created and for you to become clear about what your vision looks like and the direction to take.

It is in this direction that opportunities will be presented. Watch how you get captured by a momentum that thrives on daily routines, everyday yearning for the moment that is created through a deep love, a deep passion.

PUT THE WORK IN, STAY DISCIPLINED & BE PATIENT YOUR TIME WILL COME

6

Make Small Adjustments & Stay the Course

AS THE SEASONS CHANGE SO DO OUR
LIVES, BE IN A GROWTH MINDSET AND
ALWAYS SEEK WAYS TO EVOLVE.

Change, it's not always a welcome feeling, especially after you worked so hard for something to gain traction. After all, it's tough keeping up with the daily routines and fighting through distractions and adversity only to continue on with your dreams. You end up spending much of your time and energy on something and the last thing you want to do is stop because of some unforeseen circumstance. After a while, there builds a strong desire to be effective and protect what you started.

It all boils down to decision making and how to make the right choices. Being able to steer around those little roadblocks that pop up from time to time. Yet, there will be those times that are just simply out of our control. It is here that we need to be clear on what is controllable and what is not. You can always control how you react to something but you cannot control how something will act upon you. You can only prepare to prevent that and put yourself in the best possible position to avoid any hidden disasters.

EVERY ACTION HAS A REACTION CONTROL THE CONTROLLABLE

Understanding the controllable's is much like understanding the basic concepts of offense and defense. You can prepare yourself to manage emotions if you know what type your dealing with. Just knowing when to be aggressive and take charge and when to slow down for a moment and wait for the right timing. It takes a great deal of awareness but oddly enough when you structure your life around your vision, things become easier to manage and a bit more predictable. It's a unique and special quality that champions and some of the most successful people use to harness the ability to win.

Key Words and Definitions

A

abundance - a large quantity of something; plentifulness

adjustment - a small alteration or movement made to achieve a desired result

authentic - of undisputed origin; genuine

awareness - a knowledge or perception of a situation or fact

B

balance - a even distribution of equal proportions; stability of ones mind or feelings

blessed - endowed with divine favor and protection

breathe - the regular physiological process of taking air into the lungs and then expel it

C

center - place in the middle

change - a substitution of one thing for another; an alteration or modification

character - the mental and moral qualities distinctive to an individual

control - to exercise restraint, to hold in check

consistent - acting or done in the same way over time, especially so as to be accurate

course - the route or direction

D

defense - the action of defending from or resisting attack

desire - a strong feeling of wanting to have something or wishing for something to happen

direction - a course along which someone or something moves

E

embodies - to include or contain an expression of or give a visible form to an idea, quality or feeling

emotional space - the understanding of emotionally fueled reactions based on personality traits

energy - the strength and vitality required for the sustained physical or mental activity

engage - occupy, attract, or involve

euphoria - a feeling or state of intense excitement and happiness

E

emotional fire - passion, drama, intensity and enthusiasm

excitement - a feeling of great enthusiasm and eagerness

express yourself - to show your feeling in a particular way

extraordinary - very unusual or remarkable

F

fear - the unpleasant often strong emotion caused by anticipation or awareness of danger

fortuity - a state of being controlled by chance

G

goals - the object of a person's ambition or effect; a desired result

greatness - the quality of being great, distinguished or eminent

growth mindset - a determined feeling that ones skills and intelligence can be improved with effort and persistence. A belief pattern in which a person can get better at something by dedication of time, energy and effort

I

intentions - an act of determining mentally upon some action or result

intrinsic motivation - engaging in activity solely because you enjoy it rather than from gaining some external reward.

J

journey - a distance, course, passage or progress from one stage to another

L

lifestyle - the habits, attitudes, moral standards that constitute the mode of living of an individual or group

M

mentoring - advise or train

mindfulness - the quality in the state of being consciously aware of something

momentum - the strength or force something has when it is moving; the strength that allows something to continue or grow stronger

motivation - the general desire or willingness to do something; the reason or reasons one has for acting or behaving in a particular way

N

naturally gifted - something you find easy to do quickly and become very good at it

now moment - a period of time between the past and the future, and is associated with the events perceived directly and in the first time, not as a recollection or speculation

O

obsession - an idea or thought that continually preoccupies or intrudes a persons mind

offense - to attack or continue forward

P

passion - a strong powerful compelling emotion or feeling as love or hate

personal growth - a development that produces a person's capabilities and potential; enhance the quality of life and the realization of dreams and aspirations

personal strength - attributes that define us as individuals and are important to our growth and development

perspective - true understanding of the importance of things

pressure - the amount of force or stress applied to a point within a confined space

purity - the condition or quality of being free from anything that debases, contaminates and pollutes something

R

roadblocks - (figurative roadblock) a situation you encounter that makes it difficult or impossible to do what you want or need to do.

routine - a sequence of actions regularly followed; a fixed program

S

silence - complete absence of sound

space - the freedom and scope to live, think and develop in a way that suits one

spiritual path - the journey a conscious being makes toward living a life of high integrity and moral belief

struggle - engage in conflict; strive to achieve something in the face of difficulty or resistance

surroundings - the things and conditions around a person or thing

V

virtue - behavior showing high morale standard

vision - the ability to think about or plan the future with imagination or wisdom

W

work - activity involving mental or physical effort done in order to achieve a purpose or result

REFERENCES

McCaw, Allistair, 2016. 7 Keys to Being a Great Coach.

McCAW, Allistair. 2017. Champion Minded.

Rathbun, Ron, 1994. The Way is Within

Singer, Michael, 2007. the untethered soul.

Coyle, Daniel, 2009. The Talent Code

Iyer, Pico, 2014. The Art of Stillness, Adventures in Going Nowhere.

Reviews

A Guide to Winning in Sports, Business and in Life by Brian Jacobs

"Everyone should do a sport. It will help to improve your interpersonal skills such as patience, leadership, teamwork while relieving the main psychological issues like stress and anxiety".

Brian's quick guide is worth having if you are seeking a proper direction to shape your life achieving success in all aspects. His step-by-step tips are effective as he leaves the space to think while reading. His energy management and emotional management techniques, power of vision are fantastic tools for a balanced life. While you are making aware of them, naturally you will achieve a tranquil mind that you are longing for.

As this book is quick and simple this will attract much of school children. They are in a stage of building up their life. Hence the book will be far more advantageous. Brian skillfully blends sports skills into our day-to-day activities. By reading this book I was able to realize the importance of sports for someone's life.

Brian Jacobs' book In the Zone is a book that arrives at the right time, filled with the right messages, and aimed at the right audience! This simple layout and presentations are full of real depth of messaging and goes to the core of the guidance necessary for a young mind by providing a road map and understanding that will likely be carried by the reader through time.

Finally, a book that is instructive guide, easy to read and very motivational at many levels aimed at an audience that needs both this guidance and support.

Nand Harjani
Founder
Creative Life Sciences